CONNECT BIBLE STUDIES

The *Star Wars*® Trilogy

A New Hope
The Empire Strikes Back
Return of the Jedi
Talking about *Star Wars*®

www.connectbiblestudies.com

connect
linking the Word to the world

CONNECT BIBLE STUDIES: The *Star Wars*® Trilogy

Published by Scripture Union, 207–209 Queensway, Bletchley, MK2 2EB, England.
Scripture Union is an international Christian charity working with churches in more than 130 countries providing resources to bring the good news about Jesus Christ to children, young people and families – and to encourage them to develop spiritually through the Bible and prayer. As well as a network of volunteers, staff and associates who run holidays, church-based events and school Christian groups, Scripture Union produces a wide range of publications and supports those who use the resources through training programmes.
Email: info@scriptureunion.org.uk
Internet: www.scriptureunion.org.uk

British Library Cataloguing-in-Publication Data: a catalogue record for this book is available from the British Library.
First published 2005 ISBN 1 84427 147 1

ALSO AVAILABLE AS AN ELECTRONIC DOWNLOAD: www.connectbiblestudies.com

Cover design by Aricot Vert of Fleet, UK.

Printed and bound in the UK by CPO.

Other titles in this series:

Harry Potter 1 85999 578 0	**TV Game Shows** 1 85999 609 4
Destiny's Child: *Survivor* 1 85999 613 2	**Lord of the Rings** 1 85999 634 5
The Simpsons 1 85999 529 2	**Dido: *No Angel*** 1 85999 679 5
Sven: *On Football* 1 85999 690 6	**Pullman: *His Dark Materials*** 1 85999 714 7
Friends 1 85999 775 9	**Madonna** 1 84427 032 7
James Bond 1 84427 007 6	**John Grisham's Thrillers** 1 84427 021 1
The Matrix Trilogy 1 84427 061 0	**TV Soaps** 1 84427 087 4
Computer Animated Films 1 84427 115 3	

Titles available as electronic download only:
U2: *All That You Can't Leave Behind*/ Billy Elliot/ Chocolat/ How to be Good/ AI: Artificial Intelligence/ Iris/ Superheroes
And more titles following. Check www.connectbiblestudies.com for latest titles or ask at any good Christian bookshop.

www.connectbiblestudies.com

connect
linking the Word to the world

Using Connect Bible Studies

What Are These Studies?

These innovative home group Bible studies have two aims. Firstly, to enable group members to dig into their Bibles and get to know them better. Secondly, by being based on contemporary films, books, TV programmes, music etc, the aim is to help people think through topical issues in a biblical way.

It is not envisaged that all members will always be able to watch the films, play the music or read the books, or indeed that they will always want to. A summary is always provided. However, our vision is that knowing about these films and books empowers Christians to engage with friends and colleagues about them. Addressing issues from a biblical perspective gives Christians confidence that they know what they think, and can bring a distinctive angle to bear in conversations.

The studies are produced in sets of four – ie four weeks' worth of group Bible Study material. These are available in print published by Scripture Union from your local Christian bookshop, or via the Internet at www.connectbiblestudies.com.

How Do I Use Them?

These studies are designed to stimulate creative thought and discussion within a biblical context. Each section therefore has a range of questions or options from which you as leader may choose in order to tailor the study to your group's needs and desires. Different approaches may appeal at different times, so the studies aim to supply lots of choice. Whilst adhering to the main aim of corporate Bible study, some types of questions may enable this for your group better than others – so take your pick.

Group members should be supplied with the appropriate sheet that they can fill in, each one also showing the relevant summary.

Leader's notes contain:

1 Opening questions

These help your group settle in to discussion, while introducing the topics. They may be straightforward, personal or creative, but aim to provoke a response.

2 Summary

We suggest the summary of the book or film will follow now, read aloud if necessary. There may well be reactions that group members want to express even before getting on to the week's issue.

3 Key issue

Again, either read from the leader's notes, or summarise.

4 Scenes to watch

New for this issue Suggestions for clips to show from the relevant DVD, specially picked to tie in with the session themes. Please be aware of Copyright restrictions when showing films or excerpts from films.*

5 Bible study

Lots of choice here. Choose as appropriate to suit your group – get digging into the Bible. Background reading and texts for further help and study are suggested, but please use the material provided to inspire your group to explore their Bibles as much as possible. A concordance might be a handy standby for looking things up. A commentary could be useful too, such as the New Bible Commentary 21st Century Edition (IVP, 1994). The idea is to help people to engage with the truth of God's word, wrestling with it if necessary, but making it their own.

Don't plan to work through every question here. Within each section the two questions explore roughly the same ground but from different angles or in different ways. Our advice is to take one question from each section. The questions are open-ended so each ought to yield good discussion – though of course any discussion in a Bible study may need prompting to go a little further.

5 Implications

Here the aim is to tie together the perspectives gained through Bible study and the impact of the book or film. The implications may be personal, a change in worldview, or new ideas for relating to non-churchgoers. Choose questions that adapt to the flow of the discussion.

6 Prayer

Leave time for it! We suggest a time of open prayer, or praying in pairs if the group would prefer. Encourage your members to focus on issues from your study that had a particular impact on them. Try different approaches to prayer – light a candle, say a prayer each, write prayers down, play quiet worship music – aiming to facilitate everyone to relate to God.

All videos and DVDS are licensed for home viewing only, so it is OK to show films/excerpts in someone's home. If you want to show films/excerpts in a church setting, you will need permission or a licence. Christian Video Licensing Europe (www.CVLE.com) provides an annual licence for those wishing to show films in church, which covers an increasing number of large studios.

www.connectbiblestudies.com

connect

linking the Word to the world

A New Hope

Lucasfilm Ltd/20th Century Fox

The Star Wars® Trilogy: Part One

Han: ***What good's a reward if you ain't around to use it? Besides, attacking that battle station ain't my idea of courage. It's more like... suicide.***

Luke: ***All right. Well, take care of yourself, Han. I guess it's what you're best at, isn't it?*** [Luke turns and walks away.]

Han: ***Hey, Luke!*** [Luke looks back.] ***May the Force be with you.***

Chewbacca: [Bellows.]

Han: ***What are you looking at? I know what I'm doing.***

Please read Using Connect Bible Studies *(page 3) before leading a Bible study with this material.*

Opening Questions

Choose one of these questions.

When did you first see *Star Wars*®? Is it still as good today?	Which bit of the film did you enjoy the most?
Who's the better character: Han Solo or Luke Skywalker?	*Star Wars*® is a piece of modern mythology. Does it work that way for you?

Summary

When idealistic farm boy Luke Skywalker buys two robots, C-3P0 and R2-D2, he finds out that they are carrying a distress message from Princess Leia Organa and the secret plans of the Death Star, the evil Galactic Empire's ultimate weapon. He also discovers that the reclusive local hermit Ben Kenobi is, in fact, Obi-Wan Kenobi, former Jedi Knight and wielder of the mysterious power of the Force.

When they meet, Obi-Wan tells Luke that he is the son of Anakin Skywalker, another Jedi Knight who was murdered by Obi-Wan's former pupil Darth Vader. Luke, Obi-Wan and the droids, running the gauntlet of Imperial soldiers, buy passage on the *Millennium Falcon*, piloted by the dashing but morally dubious Han Solo and his hairy co-pilot Chewbacca. They attempt to take the plans to the planet Alderaan, only to find that the planet has been destroyed by the Death Star on the orders of the princess' captor, Grand Moff Tarkin.

The *Millennium Falcon* is dragged on board the Death Star via a tractor beam, but Luke, Han, Obi-Wan and the others manage to avoid capture. They find the princess and escape, but not without loss – Obi-Wan, finding Darth Vader on the station, faces his rebellious former pupil in a duel and sacrifices himself to allow time for the others to escape. Getting away with Princess Leia, our heroes make it to Yavin, where the Rebels analyse the plans and discover a weakness in the Death Star. The Rebels stage a desperate attack on the Death Star. Luke decides to join the pilots in the attack, but Han wants no further part and takes off in the *Millennium Falcon*.

One by one, the Rebel fighters are picked off by Imperial fighters, under the command of Darth Vader himself, until Luke is the only one left making an attack run on the Death Star's design flaw. As Luke is about to be shot down by Vader, Han returns just in time, rescuing him and giving him the time to fire the shot that destroys the Death Star. Luke, Han and Chewie return to a heroes' welcome, while Darth Vader, the Death Star's only survivor, escapes to fight again another day.

Key Issue: The courage to overcome

It's all very well dreaming of escape, but in the end, Luke Skywalker still needs to find the courage to leave home, and the faith to trust in the Force to save the day. Obi-Wan Kenobi's faith is what allows him to sacrifice himself. Han, meanwhile, has to overcome his scepticism and selfishness in order to put his friends first and play his part. All of the protagonists need to use courage and faith to get by.

Scenes to Watch

(DVD chapter references/timings in brackets)

The Force is what gives a Jedi his power... (Chapter 14 – 0:31:15)
Obi-Wan Kenobi explains to Luke Skywalker about lightsabres, the Force and the Jedi Knights in his house on Tatooine.

I've seen a lot of strange stuff... (Chapter 27 – 0:56:49).
Han Solo advances the cause of scepticism in a quiet moment on the *Millennium Falcon*.

It's more like... suicide... (Chapter 33 – 1:37:17)
Luke tries to convince Han not to leave.

If you strike me down... (Chapter 38 – 1:26:16)
Obi-Wan makes the final sacrifice. Or does he?

Bible Study

Choose one question from each section.

1 Hesitation

Obi-Wan: *I need your help Luke.* She *needs your help. I'm getting too old for this sort of thing.*

Luke: *I can't get involved. I've got work to do. It's not that I like the Empire – I hate it – but there's nothing I can do about it right now. It's all such a long way from here.*

◆ Read Judges 6:11–18 and Judges 6:36–40. Is Gideon stalling, trying to get out of his job, or just looking for reassurance?

◆ Read Isaiah 6:1–8. Are Isaiah's reservations about his worthiness justified? Does it make a difference?

2 Disbelief

Han: *Hokey religions and ancient weapons are no match for a good blaster at your side, kid.*

Luke: *You don't believe in the Force, do you?*

Han: *Kid, I've flown from one side of this galaxy to the other, and I've seen a lot of strange stuff. But I've never seen anything to make me believe that there's one all-powerful Force controlling everything. There's no mystical energy field controls my destiny. It's all a lot of simple tricks and nonsense.*

◆ Read Psalm 19:1–11. How does God show himself? How is this different to the Force?

◆ Read Psalm 104:1–18. How much evidence do you see of God in the world around you? Does it convince you? Does it convince other people? How would you argue to convince others from what you see around you?

3 Faith in a higher power

Darth Vader: *Your powers are weak, old man.*

Obi-Wan: *You can't win, Darth. If you strike me down, I shall become more powerful than you can possibly imagine.*

◆ Read Daniel 3:16–18. What's the main difference between Obi-Wan Kenobi and Shadrach, Meshach and Abednego in their approach to what looks like certain death?

◆ Read Acts 7:54–60. What would you do if you found yourself in a position where you could be killed for your faith?

4 Motives and rewards

Leia: *It's not over yet.*

Han: *It is for me, sister. Look, I ain't in this for your revolution, man. I'm not in it for you, Princess. I expect to be well paid. I'm in it for the money.*

Leia: *You needn't worry about your reward. If money is all that you love, then that's what you'll receive.*

◆ Read Matthew 6:1–4. Why is it important to have pure motives when doing good?

◆ Read Matthew 6:19–24 and 1 Timothy 6:6–10. The best-intentioned Christians can still fall prey to greed. How can we avoid this?

Implications

Admiral Motti: *Don't try to frighten us with your sorcerer's ways, Lord Vader. Your sad devotion to that ancient religion has not helped you conjure up the stolen data tapes, or given you clairvoyance enough to find the rebel's hidden fortr—* [The Admiral is cut short. He clutches at his throat, unable to breathe. Darth Vader steps forward with his hand raised.]

Darth Vader: *I find your lack of faith disturbing.*

Choose one or more of the following questions.

◆ Have you ever had to choose whether or not to leave somewhere or something behind? Did you? Did it help? Was it the right thing to do?

◆ Have you ever dreamed about being a hero? In what ways can we be heroes right here, right now?

◆ What are the similarities between what the Jedi say about the Force in the films and what Christians say about God in the real world? What are the differences? Are there more differences or similarities between the Force and God?

◆ Have you ever been hesitant to do something you should be doing because you were scared? What happened in the end?

◆ How can a Christian faith help you with your resolve?

◆ Do you ever react with scepticism when people talk about God? Why? Is it always necessarily bad to be sceptical?

◆ Is there anything in yourself which you need to overcome in order to be a better person and a better Christian?

Prayer

Spend some time praying through these issues.

Members' Sheet – *A New Hope*

connect

Summary

When idealistic farm boy Luke Skywalker buys two robots, C-3P0 and R2-D2, he finds out that they are carrying a distress message from Princess Leia Organa and the secret plans of the Death Star, the evil Galactic Empire's ultimate weapon. He also discovers that the reclusive local hermit Ben Kenobi is, in fact, Obi-Wan Kenobi, former Jedi Knight and wielder of the mysterious power of the Force.

When they meet, Obi-Wan tells Luke that he is the son of Anakin Skywalker, another Jedi Knight who was murdered by Obi-Wan's former pupil Darth Vader. Luke, Obi-Wan and the droids, running the gauntlet of Imperial soldiers, buy passage on the *Millennium Falcon*, piloted by the dashing but morally dubious Han Solo and his hairy co-pilot Chewbacca. They attempt to take the plans to the planet Alderaan, only to find that the planet has been destroyed by the Death Star on the orders of the princess' captor, Grand Moff Tarkin.

The *Millennium Falcon* is dragged on board the Death Star via a tractor beam, but Luke, Han, Obi-Wan and the others manage to avoid capture. They find the princess and escape, but not without loss – Obi-Wan, finding Darth Vader on the station, faces his rebellious former pupil in a duel and sacrifices himself to allow time for the others to escape. Getting away with Princess Leia, our heroes make it to Yavin, where the Rebels analyse the plans and discover a weakness in the Death Star. The Rebels stage a desperate attack on the Death Star. Luke decides to join the pilots in the attack, but Han wants no further part and takes off in the *Millennium Falcon*.

One by one, the Rebel fighters are picked off by Imperial fighters, led by Darth Vader himself, until Luke is the only one left making an attack run on the Death Star's design flaw. As Luke is about to be shot down by Vader, Han returns just in time, rescuing him and giving him the time to fire the shot that destroys the Death Star. Luke, Han and Chewie return to a heroes' welcome, while Darth Vader, the Death Star's only survivor, escapes to fight again another day.

Key Issue

Bible Study notes

Implications

Prayer

www.connectbiblestudies.com

connect
linking the Word to the world

The Empire Strikes Back

Lucasfilm Ltd/20th Century Fox

The *Star Wars*® Trilogy: Part Two

Obi-Wan's Ghost: ***It is you and your abilities the Emperor wants.***
That is why your friends are made to suffer.
Luke: ***That is why I must go to them.***

Please read Using Connect Bible Studies *(page 3) before leading a Bible study with this material.*

Opening Questions

Choose one of these questions.

A lot of critics and fans think that *The Empire Strikes Back* is the best of the *Star Wars*® films. Do you think so?	Does it bother you that *The Empire Strikes Back* doesn't have a happy ending?
What makes *The Empire Strikes Back* different from the first film?	Where would you rather spend a week: Hoth, Dagobah or Bespin?

Summary

Hiding out at the Rebel base on the desolate ice-planet of Hoth, Luke Skywalker falls foul of a carnivorous beast while on a routine patrol. Although he escapes, he is confronted by the ghost of Obi-Wan Kenobi during his ordeal, who tells him to travel to Dagobah and seek out Yoda, who will train him in the skills he needs to be a Jedi Knight. But Luke's preparations for leaving are interrupted by news that the Empire has tracked the Rebel base down.

After fighting a desperate retreat against the Empire's unstoppable war machine, the friends are separated: Luke and R2-D2 travel to Dagobah, while Han Solo, Princess Leia, C-3P0 and Chewbacca find themselves forced to escape the Empire's increasingly dogged pursuit in the damaged and faulty *Millennium Falcon*. While hiding out, Han and Leia begin to realise their feelings for one another. Meanwhile, on the swamp planet of Dagobah, Luke finds a small irritable creature who offers to lead him to Yoda. Discovering that the small alien actually is Yoda himself, Luke begins training.

Han and Leia manage to make it to Bespin, where, landing on Cloud City, they are met by Han's old friend and former owner of the *Millennium Falcon*, Lando Calrissian, now governor of a mining colony. However, the Empire is already there and, against his will, Lando has been forced by Darth Vader and his hired hand Boba Fett to deliver Han and Leia to them – Vader intends to use them as bait to trap Luke. Han Solo is frozen into a block of carbonite, and taken by Boba Fett to the home of the crime lord Jabba the Hutt, who has a bounty out on Han.

Luke, terrified by visions of his friends in danger, decides to cut short his training and go to them, against the advice of Yoda and Obi-Wan's ghost. He finds his way to Bespin, where he is confronted by Darth Vader. They fight a lightsaber duel. Luke, outmatched and defeated, is told by Vader that Obi-Wan lied and that he is actually Anakin Skywalker, Luke's father. Luke, unable to cope with this revelation, throws himself down a ventilation shaft and ends up hanging desperately from the underside of Cloud City. Lando, in a change of heart, helps Leia, Chewie, C-3PO and R2-D2 to escape on the *Falcon*. As they're flying away, Leia gets a feeling that they have to go back to help Luke, and they arrive just in time. They pull him on board the *Falcon* and escape the Empire. Back at the Rebel Fleet, Luke tries to cope with his new knowledge, while Lando and Chewbacca begin their search for Han.

Key Issue: The ties that bind

Friendship, love, loyalty, duty, blood: all of these ties come into play and into conflict in *The Empire Strikes Back*. Han risks his life to look for Luke in the wastes of icy Hoth. Luke's duty to his calling as a Jedi Knight is sorely tested when the lives of those he loves are at stake. Han and Leia find love, and it's Han's love for Leia and his faith in his friends which allow him to let himself be taken away – he knows they'll find him. But ties can be exploited, too. Han's friendship with Lando Calrissian allows him to fall into Darth Vader's trap; and when Vader reveals the truth to Luke about their real relationship, Luke's entire world is shaken.

Scenes to Watch

(DVD chapter references/timings in brackets)

What's in there? (Chapter 28 – 0:58:28)
Luke experiences a strange ordeal inside a cave, and learns that what you take with you is what you get.

Do, or do not. There is no try... (Chapter 31 – 1:05:25)
Yoda shows Luke that size really doesn't matter.

I love you! (Chapter 40 – 1:30:47)
Han faces his fate with dignity (and delivers one of the best lines in the entire saga).

I am your father... (Chapter 46 – 1:44:54)
Darth Vader reveals the truth, and Luke chooses almost certain death over turning to the Dark Side.

Bible Study

Choose one question from each section.

1 A conflict of interests

Luke: ***I've got to go to them.***

Yoda: ***Decide you must how to serve them best. If you leave now, help them you could, but you will destroy all for which they have fought and suffered.***

◆ Read John 15:12,13. If you had a choice between duty to your religion and duty to your friends, what would you do?

◆ Read Mark 7:5–12. Have you ever used your religious faith as an excuse to get out of fulfilling your duty to your family and friends?

Note for leaders: The practice of Corban was originally a way for people to pledge their skills, time and possessions to the temple. By Jesus' time, people had begun to exploit a loophole in the system as a means of escaping familial obligations. It was this exploitation of the system that Jesus was criticising.

2 Letting them down

Lando: ***I had no choice. They arrived right before you did. I'm sorry.***

Han: ***I'm sorry, too.***

◆ Read Mark 14:66–72. What does it feel like when you know you've betrayed someone important to you?

◆ Read Jonah 1:1–10. Have you ever found it hard to admit when you've failed or betrayed God or someone else?

3 The ugly truth

Darth Vader: ***If you only knew the power of the Dark Side. Obi-Wan never told you what happened to your father.***

Luke: ***He told me enough! He told me you killed him!***

Darth Vader: ***No. I am your father.***

Luke: ***No! No! That's not true! That's impossible!***

Darth Vader: ***Search your feelings. You know it to be true.***

Luke: [Screams.] ***Noooooo!***

◆ Read 2 Kings 22:8–20. Sometimes learning the truth about yourself can be a difficult experience. What's the best way to react to difficult truths? What does Josiah do?

◆ Read John 8:31,32. Do you feel that you know the truth? Has it set you free? Is this your experience? Why? Or, if it isn't, why not? What did he learn about his father?

4 Faith in your friends

Han: *Stop, Chewie! Hey! Hey! Listen to me! Chewie! Chewie! This won't help me! Hey! Save your strength. There'll be another time. The Princess – you have to take care of her. You hear me? Huh?* [Chewbacca calms down. The Stormtroopers move to take Han away. Han and Leia kiss, but they are pulled apart.]

Leia: *I love you.*

Han: *I know.*

◆ Read Philemon 8–21. Why does Paul trust Onesimus and Philemon?

◆ Read Acts 4:32–37. How should Christians support each other? Is this your own experience of how Christians behave?

Implications

Yoda: **Size matters not. Look at me! Judge me by my size, do you? Hmmm. And well you should not. For my ally is the Force.**

Choose one or more of the following questions.

◆ Has your faith ever got in the way of your relationships with friends and family? What did you do?

◆ In what ways does the Jedi religion parallel Christianity? How is it different?

◆ What would be your attitude if you found out that your real father or mother was a thief or a murderer (or Darth Vader, for that matter)? What would you do?

◆ Would you want Yoda or Obi-Wan Kenobi as teachers? If yes, why? If no, who would you rather get your spiritual guidance from? Why?

◆ To what or whom do you give your loyalty?

◆ What do you look for in a friend?

◆ How far would you go for your friends? Do you find it difficult to trust your friends to come through for you?

◆ Should friendships between Christians be different to friendships between non-Christians?

Prayer

Spend some time praying through these issues.

Members' Sheet – *The Empire Strikes Back*

Summary

Hiding out at the Rebel base on the desolate ice-planet of Hoth, Luke Skywalker falls foul of a carnivorous beast while on a routine patrol. Although he escapes, he is confronted by the ghost of Obi-Wan Kenobi during his ordeal, who tells him to travel to Dagobah and seek out Yoda, who will train him in the skills he needs to be a Jedi Knight. But Luke's preparations for leaving are interrupted by news that the Empire has tracked the Rebel base down.

After fighting a desperate retreat against the Empire's unstoppable war machine, the friends are separated: Luke and R2-D2 travel to Dagobah, while Han Solo, Princess Leia, C-3P0 and Chewbacca find themselves forced to escape the Empire's increasingly dogged pursuit in the damaged and faulty *Millennium Falcon*. While hiding out, Han and Leia begin to realise their feelings for one another. Meanwhile, on the swamp planet of Dagobah, Luke finds a small irritable creature who offers to lead him to Yoda. Discovering that the small alien actually is Yoda himself, Luke begins training.

Han and Leia manage to make it to Bespin, where, landing on Cloud City, they are met by Han's old friend and former owner of the *Millennium Falcon*, Lando Calrissian, now governor of a mining colony. However, the Empire is already there and, against his will, Lando has been forced by Darth Vader and his hired hand Boba Fett to deliver Han and Leia to them – Vader intends to use them as bait to trap Luke. Han Solo is frozen into a block of carbonite, and taken by Boba Fett to the home of the crime lord Jabba the Hutt, who has a bounty out on Han.

Luke, terrified by visions of his friends in danger, decides to cut short his training and go to them, against the advice of Yoda and Obi-Wan's ghost. He finds his way to Bespin, where he is confronted by Darth Vader. They fight a lightsaber duel. Luke, outmatched and defeated, is told by Vader that Obi-Wan lied and that he is actually Anakin Skywalker, Luke's father. Luke, unable to cope with this revelation, throws himself down a ventilation shaft, and ends up hanging desperately from the underside of Cloud City. Lando, in a change of heart, helps Leia, Chewie, C-3P0 and R2-D2 to escape on the *Falcon*. As they're flying away, Leia gets a feeling that they have to go back to help Luke, and they arrive just in time. They pull him on board the *Falcon* and escape the Empire. Back at the Rebel Fleet, Luke tries to cope with his new knowledge, while Lando and Chewbacca begin their search for Han.

Key Issue

Bible Study notes

Implications

Prayer

www.connectbiblestudies.com

connect
linking the Word to the world

Return of the Jedi

Lucasfilm Ltd/20th Century Fox

The *Star Wars*® Trilogy: Part Three

The Emperor: ***His compassion for you will be his undoing. He will come to you and then you will bring him before me.***
Darth Vader: ***As you wish.***

Please read Using Connect Bible Studies *(page 3) before leading a Bible study with this material.*

Opening Questions

Choose one of these questions.

Which aspect do you most enjoy: the drama or the action and special effects?	Do you like the Ewoks?
Like Luke, have you ever returned to a place you didn't want to go back to?	Why do you think the *Star Wars*® trilogy has hit such a chord with so many people?

Summary

In a finely-managed operation back on Tatooine, Luke, Leia, Lando, Chewie and the droids rescue Han from the clutches of Jabba the Hutt. Luke then returns to Dagobah to discover from Obi-Wan's ghost that Darth Vader told the truth about being his father, and also that Leia is his twin sister. Yoda dies, but not before telling Luke he must face his father.

Luke joins up with his friends again at the Rebel Fleet, where it is revealed that the Empire is building a second Death Star. The Rebels have found its location and have discovered that the Emperor himself is supervising its construction.

Lando leads a space-borne assault on the Death Star while the others join a commando team sent to the nearby forest moon of Endor in order to destroy the generator powering the Death Star's energy shields. The Rebels face huge opposition, but they're aided by the planet's natives, the small furry Ewoks, who they befriend after a small misunderstanding about C-3PO being a god.

Luke, realising that Darth Vader knows he is there through the power of the Force, turns himself in to the Imperials. Taken up to the Death Star, Luke is forced by the Emperor, himself a twisted Jedi Knight, to fight his father. Defeating Vader but refusing to kill him, Luke is tortured nearly to the point of death by the Emperor's powers. But Darth Vader, redeemed by the love of his son, saves Luke and kills the Emperor, becoming mortally wounded in the process. With his last words, Darth Vader renounces evil and removes his mask to look upon his son with his own eyes for the first and last time. Then he dies. Luke escapes from the Death Star as the Rebels triumph both in space and on Endor, and the Empire's centre of power is destroyed.

There are celebrations all over the galaxy as the news gets out. Han and Leia declare their love for each other once more, and Luke is comforted by the ghosts of Obi-Wan Kenobi, Yoda and his father, Anakin Skywalker.

Key Issue: Love conquers

Love, mercy, compassion: all of these are demonstrated in the last film in the saga. Han's friends come through for him, every one of them – even Lando – putting their lives on the line to rescue him from the clutches of Jabba the Hutt. Han and Leia's relationship grows and develops, and Luke's affection for Leia uncovers a secret they never knew. And despite the advice of both Yoda and Obi-Wan, the plans of the Emperor, and Darth Vader's denials, Luke's unearned love for his father does win through, and the trilogy ends with Anakin Skywalker finding final redemption.

Scenes to Watch

(DVD chapter references/timings in brackets)

I never knew I had it in me... (Chapter 25 – 1:09:04)
C-3PO finally does something useful.

I will not turn, and you will be forced to kill me... (Chapter 28 – 1:19:08)
Luke turns himself in.

If you will not turn to the Dark Side, then perhaps she will... (Chapter 41 – 1:47:03)
Darth Vader discovers the one thing that goads Luke into fighting.

You were right about me... (Chapter 46 – 1:54:40)
Luke removes Darth Vader's mask; Anakin Skywalker dies.

Bible Study

Choose one question from each section.

1 Deception

Luke: ***Why didn't you tell me? You told me Vader betrayed and murdered my father!***

Obi-Wan's Ghost: ***Your father was seduced by the Dark Side of the Force. He ceased to be Anakin Skywalker and became Darth Vader. When that happened, the good man who was your father was destroyed. So what I told you was true, from a certain point of view.***

Luke: ***A certain point of view?***

Obi-Wan's Ghost: ***Luke, you're going to find that many of the truths we cling to depend greatly on our own point of view.***

◆ Read Genesis 12:10–20. Abram's dishonesty was borne out of concern for his family. It didn't work out. Have you ever found yourself avoiding the truth for what seemed to you to be the right reasons? How did it work out for you?

◆ Read Exodus 1:15–20. Is it ever acceptable to lie? Under what circumstances?

2 Broken families

Luke: ***Do you remember your mother – your real mother?***

Leia: ***Just a little bit. She died when I was very young.***

Luke: ***What do you remember?***

Leia: ***Just images, really. Feelings ... She was very beautiful. Kind... but sad. Why are you asking me this?***

Luke: ***I have no memory of my mother. I never knew her.***

◆ Read Psalm 27:7–14. Have you ever found yourself abandoned or left behind – whether deliberately or not – by someone dear to you? How did it feel? Do these verses help you?

◆ Read John 14:15–21. Can Jesus heal the wounds left by bereavement or abandonment? Does it work that way? What would you say to someone who has been bereaved or abandoned? Would it help?

3 Compassion for the lost

Leia: ***But why must you confront him?***

Luke: ***Because there is good in him. I've felt it. He won't turn me over to the Emperor. I can save him. I can turn him back to the Good Side. I have to try.***

◆ Read Luke 15:1–7. What does it feel like when someone you really care for is 'lost' to you?

◆ Read Luke 15:8–10. Is there ever any reason for us to give up on someone?

4   Resisting the lure of the Dark Side

Luke: *I'll never turn to the Dark Side. You've failed, your highness. I am a Jedi – like my father before me.*
The Emperor: *So be it. Jedi.*

◆   Read 1 Corinthians 10:12,13. Why shouldn't you be concerned when you are tempted to do wrong? Why should you?

◆   Read Ephesians 6:10–18. What resources does God give us to enable us to stand firm? How do these work out in everyday life? How do we use them?

Implications

Luke: *You're coming with me. I'll not leave you here. I've got to save you!*
Anakin: *You already have Luke. You were right... you were right about me. Tell your sister... you were right.*

Choose one or more of the following questions.

◆   Do you think that the *Star Wars*® films present an accurate picture of the battle between good and evil?

◆   What's your own experience of the battle against evil? Can you see any parallels between the *Star Wars*® films and your own life?

◆   Could you have gone as far as Luke Skywalker did in order to try to save a person as apparently irredeemable as Darth Vader?

◆   Have you ever found yourself not wanting to accept friendship or help from someone who doesn't appear to have much to offer? How did that work out?

◆   To what extent do Luke Skywalker's actions in *Return of the Jedi* mirror the behaviour expected of a Christian? What's different?

◆   Have you ever found it difficult to relate to your parents?

◆   Do you know anyone with a family that has become estranged or separated by circumstance? What can you do to help families who suffer in this way? What if it's your family?

◆   What would you say to someone who is thinking of giving up on their family and friends? What if they're a Christian?

Prayer

Spend some time praying through these issues.

Members' Sheet – *Return of the Jedi*

Summary

In a finely-managed operation back on Tatooine, Luke, Leia, Lando, Chewie and the droids rescue Han from the clutches of Jabba the Hutt. Luke then returns to Dagobah to discover from Obi-Wan's ghost that Darth Vader told the truth about being his father, and also that Leia is his twin sister. Yoda dies, but not before telling Luke he must face his father.

Luke joins up with his friends again at the Rebel Fleet, where it is revealed that the Empire is building a second Death Star. The Rebels have found its location and have discovered that the Emperor himself is supervising its construction.

Lando leads a space-borne assault on the Death Star while the others join a commando team sent to the nearby forest moon of Endor in order to destroy the generator powering the Death Star's energy shields. The Rebels face huge opposition, but they're aided by the planet's natives, the small furry Ewoks, who they befriend after a small misunderstanding about C-3PO being a god.

Luke, realising that Darth Vader knows he is there through the power of the Force, turns himself in to the Imperials. Taken up to the Death Star, Luke is forced by the Emperor, himself a twisted Jedi Knight, to fight his father. Defeating Vader but refusing to kill him, Luke is tortured nearly to the point of death by the Emperor's powers. But Darth Vader, redeemed by the love of his son, saves Luke and kills the Emperor, becoming mortally wounded in the process. With his last words, Darth Vader renounces evil and removes his mask to look upon his son with his own eyes for the first and last time. Then he dies. Luke escapes from the Death Star as the Rebels triumph both in space and on Endor, and the Empire's centre of power is destroyed.

There are celebrations all over the galaxy as the news gets out. Han and Leia declare their love for each other once more, and Luke is comforted by the ghosts of Obi-Wan Kenobi, Yoda and his father, Anakin Skywalker.

Key Issue

Bible Study notes

Implications

Prayer

Talking about *Star Wars®*

Lucasfilm Ltd/20th Century Fox

The *Star Wars®* Trilogy: Part Four

Yoda: ***Do, or do not – there is no try.*** (*The Empire Strikes Back*)

Silent Bob: ***Do, or do not – there is no try.*** (*Chasing Amy*)

Please read Using Connect Bible Studies *(page 3) before leading a Bible study with this material.*

Opening Questions

Choose one of these questions.

Did you own any *Star Wars®* toys/merchandise when you were a kid? Do you own any now?	Have you ever found yourself quoting from *Star Wars®* in everyday conversation?
Do you think that the *Star Wars®* films deserve their place in the pop culture canon?	Have you ever been influenced in your moral decisions by a film?

Summary

In this age of hundreds of TV channels and consumer choice, it's difficult to imagine the effect that the very first *Star Wars®* film had on people. There were queues around the block for weeks on end, making it the very first film to be described as a 'blockbuster'. Every Hollywood action movie since owes it a debt, either directly or indirectly, from *Die Hard* to *Raiders of the Lost Ark* to *The Matrix* to *Gladiator* – in terms of plot development, music, dialogue and many other things. The original *Star Wars®* trilogy has become a pop-culture classic. If you're between the ages of 25 and 40, you're more than likely to have seen it, and the prequel trilogy, along with the Special Edition re-releases of the original films in 1997 (in the cinema and on video) and in

2004 (on DVD), all of which have introduced *Star Wars*® to successive generations. It's very likely that there will never again be a phenomenon to match it.

Many of the people who were kids when they saw the *Star Wars*® trilogy the first time around have now grown up to be film-makers themselves, and it's no surprise that other films directly reference *Star Wars*® in their dialogue. Mel Brooks' 1987 film *Spaceballs* satirises the merchandising juggernaut that the *Star Wars*® films quickly became.

Meanwhile, film-maker Kevin Smith, whose films tend to be about members of the *Star Wars*® generation, has often included visual references and dialogue about the *Star Wars*® films and the questions they raise. In this study, we'll be looking at some film scenes which reference the *Star Wars*® trilogy.

Key Issue: How do we watch films?

How much does the media we consume affect us? To what extent do we draw our morality from the films we watch? How do these films match up with our own compass of what is right and what is wrong? And, if we're Christians, how much should popular culture influence our lives?

Scenes to Watch

(DVD chapter references/timings in brackets)

No disintegrations...

(*The Empire Strikes Back*, Chapter 30, 1:03:06)
The first appearance of Boba Fett in the *Star Wars*® trilogy. How did a character who only has a few lines get turned into such a popular character/action figure?

'Up until that time, merchandising had been relatively unknown...'

(*Star Wars*® DVD Bonus Disk documentary – *Empire of Dreams*, Chapter 1 – 0:17:20)
20th Century Fox underestimates the appeal of merchandising and George Lucas 'changes the world'.

A small army of fans had been building...

(*Star Wars*® DVD Bonus Disk documentary – *Empire of Dreams*, Chapter 5 – 1:12:00)
How the first film found its audience and became a pop culture phenomenon.

Bible Study

Choose one question from each section.

1   Merchandising

Yoghurt: ***Merchandising! Merchandising, where the real money from the movie is made!
Spaceballs –*** *the T-shirt!* **Spaceballs –** *the Colouring Book!* **Spaceballs –** *the
Lunch Box!* **Spaceballs –** *the Breakfast Cereal!* **Spaceballs –** *the Flame Thrower!*
[Picks up flame thrower and turns it on.]***... The kids love this one.*** [A Dink hands
Yoghurt a doll that looks just like him.] ***And last but not least,*** **Spaceballs –** *the
Doll. Me!* [Pulls string.]

Doll: ***May the Schwartz be with you!***   (*Spaceballs*)

◆   Read Luke 12:32–34. What possessions do you have which you really value? What
matters to you the most?

◆   Read Luke 18:18–30. If you were asked to give away all your possessions... could you?

2   Making it say what you want it to say

Hooper: ***Always some white boy gotta invoke the Holy Trilogy! Bust this: those movies
are about how the white man keeps the brother man down... even in a galaxy
far, far away.***   (*Chasing Amy*)

◆   People have a tendency to read whatever meanings they want into things – *Star Wars* ®
is a common victim of this. Read Genesis 40:1–22. How can we know what
something means... and what it's really supposed to mean (rather than what we want it
to mean)?

◆   Read Luke 18:31–34. Can you think of some reasons why the disciples didn't
understand what Jesus had to say here? Do you think they wanted to understand?
Leaders: hint – see Matthew 16:21–23.

3   Real life

Randal: ***Which did you like better:*** **Jedi** *or* **The Empire Strikes Back?**
Dante: **Empire.**
Randal: ***Blasphemy!***
Dante: **Empire** *had the better ending: Luke gets his hand cut off, and finds out Vader's
his father; Han gets frozen and taken away by Boba Fett. It ends on such a
down note. And that's life – a series of down endings. All* **Jedi** *had was a bunch
of muppets.* (*Clerks*)

◆   Read Luke 21:25–28. Why should Jesus present his disciples with such bad news? It's
not exactly a sales pitch, is it?

◆   Read 1 Peter 2:18–21. How does Christianity compare with modern cinema in how it
presents real life?

4 Things are less complicated in Hollywood

Dante: *All right. So even if independent contractors were working on the Death Star, why are you uneasy with its destruction?*

Randal: *All those innocent contractors hired to do a job were killed – casualties of a war they had nothing to do with. All right, look. You're a roofer and some juicy government contract comes your way. You got the wife and kids and the two-storey in suburbia – this is a government contract, which means all sorts of benefits. All of a sudden these left-wing militants blast you with lasers and wipe out everything in a three-mile radius. You didn't ask for that. You have no personal politics. You were just trying to scrape out a living.* (Clerks)

◆ Read Job 1:13–20. Hollywood often seems to ignore the greater implications of violent actions for the sake of making a fun movie. How should we react to the suffering of other people, whether it's those we love or complete strangers?

◆ Read Luke 13:1–5. Does Jesus ignore innocent victims? Should we?

Implications

Daisy: *So how are you?*
Tim: *I'm good, I'm good. Just... had a few things to sort out.*
Daisy: *With Sarah?*
Tim: *No, with George Lucas.*
Daisy: *Tim, it's been over a year.*
Tim: *It's been 18 months, Daisy. And it still hurts.*
Daisy: *Well, I didn't think* The Phantom Menace *was that bad.* (Spaced)

Choose one or more of the following questions.

◆ Do you think that cinema affects the way we think?

◆ Do you agree with the morality in the *Star Wars* ® films?

◆ Do you think that it's possible to treat the *Star Wars* ® films as an inspirational source for living a Christian life? Should you? Why? Why not?

◆ How useful is it really to compare the *Star Wars* ® films to what Scripture says?

◆ What would you say to someone who filled in the 'religion' box in his census form with 'Jedi'?

◆ Do secular films/books/TV ever affect the way you approach your Christian faith?

◆ Which is better, Christian media or secular media?

Prayer

Spend some time praying through these issues.

Members' Sheet – Talking about *Star Wars*®

Summary

In this age of hundreds of TV channels and consumer choice, it's difficult to imagine the effect that the very first *Star Wars*® film had on people. There were queues around the block for weeks on end, making it the very first film to be described as a 'blockbuster'. Every Hollywood action movie since owes it a debt, either directly or indirectly, from *Die Hard* to *Raiders of the Lost Ark* to *The Matrix* to *Gladiator* – in terms of plot development, music, dialogue and many other things. The original *Star Wars*® trilogy has become a pop-culture classic. If you're between the ages of 25 and 40, you're more than likely to have seen it, and the prequel trilogy, along with the Special Edition re-releases of the original films in 1997 (in the cinema and on video) and in 2004 (on DVD), all of which have introduced *Star Wars*® to successive generations. It's very likely that there will never again be a phenomenon to match it.

Many of the people who were kids when they saw the *Star Wars*® trilogy the first time around have now grown up to be film-makers themselves, and it's no surprise that other films directly reference *Star Wars*® in their dialogue. Mel Brooks' 1987 film *Spaceballs* satirises the merchandising juggernaut that the *Star Wars*® films quickly became.

Meanwhile, film-maker Kevin Smith, whose films tend to be about members of the *Star Wars*® generation, has often included visual references and dialogue about the *Star Wars*® films and the questions they raise. In this study, we'll be looking at some film scenes which reference the *Star Wars*® trilogy.

Key Issue

Bible Study notes

Implications

Prayer